EMERGENCE OF CRYPTOCURRENCY, PROSPECTS AND CHALLENGES TO NATIONAL FISCAL POLICIES AND THE ECONOMY.

OGUDO ADAOBI CHINENYE

ISBN:

DEDICATION

This book is dedicated to all the people who inspired me to write this book.

CONTENTS

ACKNOWLEDGMENTS

I acknowledge all those who made it possible to write this book.

CHAPTER 1

INTRODUCTION

Cryptocurrency is a new type of currency that has been circulating the market over the years raising all kinds of speculations and fears about its operation and trade. Some individuals see cryptocurrency as a future payment while many still have little or no idea about cryptocurrency and its transaction.

Across the world, not much is known about cryptocurrency and some countries do not have a big cryptocurrency market. After a few countries legalized cryptocurrency more countries are warming up to the idea of adopting cryptocurrency. Some businesses have adopted cryptocurrency technology in their transaction.

In most countries, over the years the government has not had much knowledge of cryptocurrency and its transaction. Over the years, some countries ban bitcoin transactions due to no regulations to checkmate and monitor cryptocurrency transactions and trade in their country. Many people who transacted cryptocurrencies were not happy with the ban and sought other ways to transact cryptocurrencies. There was a push from cryptocurrency users for the legalization of cryptocurrency in their countries. Meanwhile, some countries introduced cryptocurrency regulations to guide and control cryptocurrency transactions in their country.

CHAPTER 2

HISTORICAL BACKGROUND OF CRYPTOCURRENCY

The history of cryptocurrencies can be traced back to the 1980s when they were called cyber currencies. These coins started gaining in popularity in 2008 with the introduction of Bitcoin which was created by an anonymous programmer or group of programmers under the name Satoshi Nakamoto.

Since the launch of Bitcoin in 2009, cryptocurrency has been all the rage. Over the past few years, their popularity has only grown with more and more people investing in them.

Mainstream payment processing platforms such as PayPal have introduced features for buying and selling cryptocurrencies, Bitcoin, and Ethereum, and in some cases using them as payment.

Cryptocurrencies are digital assets that use cryptography to secure and verify transactions in a network. Cryptography is also used to manage and control the creation of such currencies. Cryptography is simply the encryption of data.

Cryptocurrencies are decentralized and privately owned while digital currency is owned and controlled by the government. Bitcoin and Ethereum are examples of cryptocurrencies. Depending on the jurisdiction, cryptocurrencies may or may not be regulated.

Cryptocurrency runs on blockchain technology. A blockchain is a digitally distributed, decentralized public ledger that exists across a network. It is most noteworthy in its use with cryptocurrencies and Non-fungible tokens NFTs. Also, blockchain is a secured type of ledger or spreadsheet. Blockchain records and organizes transactions into a series of blocks. Every time you pay for something with bitcoin that transaction is recorded as a block.

Each block contains transaction data that consist of who was paid and how much was paid, the hash which is the unique identifier or public key (1b40529467385), and the previous hash block sequence or the last transaction that was recorded.

The blocks are connected. If something in a block is changed, a hash is changed in the block and subsequent blocks do not have a matching hash which affects the blocks making the blocks invalid. To hack cryptocurrency, the hash in all the blocks in the networks worldwide has to match and be consistent, this can be done by going into all the computers or networks worldwide to tamper with the blocks which are impossible to execute, therefore hacking the blockchain will be difficult

CHAPTER 3

PRICE DETERMINANT OF CRYPTOCURRENCY

The price of cryptocurrency is determined by speculations. They are tied to the news cycle when a glowing article is published about cryptocurrency the price goes up but when a negative tweet is made about cryptocurrency, the price goes down. Also, the forces of demand and supply influence the price of cryptocurrency as a result of this the price of cryptocurrency fluctuates. The price of cryptocurrency is also influenced by the following:

I, **Cost Of Production:** New cryptocurrency tokens are produced through a process called mining. Mining for cryptocurrency involves using a computer to verify the next block on the blockchain. Verifying the blockchain requires computing power. Participants invest in expensive equipment and electricity to mine cryptocurrency. As mining costs increase it necessitates an increased value of the cryptocurrency.

Ii, **Cryptocurrency Exchanges:** Some smaller tokens may only be available on select exchanges, thus limiting access for some investors. If a cryptocurrency becomes listed on more exchanges it can increase the number of investors willing and able to buy it, thus increasing demand. As demand increases, the price goes up.

Iii, **Competition**: The number of existing cryptocurrencies just keeps increasing, with new tokens being launched every day. There are meme coins, soccer team coins, celebrity coins, and many more. There are also viable cryptocurrency projects among these new coins that could overcome a current limitation and build a strong user network and competitive price

CHAPTER 4

PROSPECTS OF CRYPTOCURRENCY TO NATIONAL FISCAL POLICIES AND THE ECONOMY

A. Cheaper trade and transaction cost: Some of the advantages of cryptocurrencies are that they enable seamless transfer of value and can make transactions cheaper. With cryptocurrency transactions, there are zero or low transfer fees. Cryptocurrency transfer fees in exchanges range from 0.1% to 1%. Cryptocurrency ease business transaction because of the low cost of transfer fee. Also, cryptocurrency offers fast payment processing. There are no exchange rates or interest rates in cryptocurrency transactions. The Government will incur less budget deficit on public expenditures such as the cost of infrastructure, healthcare, education, etc if cryptocurrency is used for public spending on local and international transactions. In the future, the government may likely use cryptocurrencies such as bitcoin or digital currency to pay for public expenditure on infrastructure, healthcare, education, and the military.

B. Ease business transaction and payment: There are no intermediary financial institutions to execute transactions; only the internet and computer are needed. Cryptocurrency can ease the implementation of monetary and fiscal policy. Under the current currency regime, the federal and state governments work through a series of intermediaries' banks, and financial institutions to circulate money into the economy. Cryptocurrency can help circumvent this mechanism and enable government agencies to disburse payments directly to citizens.

C. Ease movement of money: Cryptocurrency also simplifies the production and distribution methods by obviating the need for physical manufacturing and transportation of currency notes from one location to another.

D. Ease international payment problems with forex: Cryptocurrency eases online purchases and payments. Some suppliers on popular E-commerce sites such as Alibaba accept bitcoin for payment in exchange for their products. Some countries are experiencing a scarcity of forex for international transactions and as such have imposed monthly dollar spending limits on the local currency credit cards and debit cards for international transactions in online stores. Cryptocurrency can be used to substitute credit cards and debit cards and make payments online without any spending limit. Cryptocurrency can solve the forex problem financial institutions and other commercial banks are facing.

E. <u>Provision of stimulus fund and financial benefits:</u> Sometimes, cryptocurrency can provide free money or financial benefit for its holders or investors. Often, when a new crypto coin or token is launched, the company that launched the new crypto coin will give out free crypto coins worth about a hundred US dollars $100 to the public who participated in the initial coin offering (ICO). This free crypto coin distribution is a stimulus fund for the disadvantaged.

The table shows the number of daily transactions on the blockchain in Bitcoin and Ethereum and four (4) other cryptocurrencies from August 2021 to November 2021

Characteristics Date	Binance (BNB)	Bitcoin (BTC)	Ethereum (ETH)	Litecoin (LTC)	Ripple (XRP)	Tether (USDT)
August 2021	-	273,720	1,206,314	155,189	1,122,290	523
September 2021	-	289,577	1,116,157	133,472	1,320,182	315
October 2021	-	216,741	1,304,184	134,021	2,075,839	312
November 01, 2021	-	289,324	1,341,733	148,085	1,938,573	307
November 02, 2021	-	300,911	1,395,656	152,555	1,962,044	430
November 03, 2021	-	290,879	1,417,221	150,784	1,464,852	484
November 04, 2021	-	286,047	1,352,186	139,720	1,259,841	422
November 05, 2021	-	282,446	1,339,661	133,753	1,334,595	444
November 06, 2021	-	237,201	1,255,921	135,986	1,909,358	282
November 07, 2021	-	222,930	1,276,998	134,298	2,221,167	201

As seen from the table above, cryptocurrencies have a high volume of transactions. Cryptocurrency transactions will continue to increase in the future. Transaction volume recorded on a peer-to-peer cryptocurrency exchange called Local Bitcoins revealed that in the fourth quarter of the year 2020,

Nigeria became the 5th largest cryptocurrency market by trading volume knocking out the USA from its previous place.

Recently, some countries such as Nigeria, Central Africa Republic, Mexico, Chile, El Salvador, Japan etc introduced new cryptocurrency regulations to manage the risk of cryptocurrency price volatility and classifying cryptocurrency as "securities" Nigeria is likely to remove the ban or restrictions on financial institutions prohibiting them from facilitating cryptocurrency transactions in Nigeria. Soon, it is likely that financial institutions in those countries will begin to facilitate cryptocurrency transactions and more countries where cryptocurrency is banned or restricted will lift the ban and restriction, more people across the world will make use of cryptocurrency for trade and payment.

CHAPTER 5

CHALLENGES OF CRYPTOCURRENCY TO FISCAL POLICIES AND THE ECONOMY

i. Price volatility: Some countries such as the United States of America, United Kingdom, Italy, India, Canada, and Germany tax cryptocurrency trade. Some of the disadvantages of cryptocurrencies are that they can be volatile to trade. The price volatility of cryptocurrency may not be a good source of generating public revenue through trade and taxation. Tax is levied on the profit made from the cryptocurrency trade. If the price of cryptocurrency decline, losses are made and tax cannot be generated.

ii. Tax Evasion: Since cryptocurrency is decentralized and not controlled by intermediary financial institutions or the government, tax can be evaded when a crypto trader makes a profit from cryptocurrency trade. Although some countries banned cryptocurrency transactions trading still goes on through peer-to-peer transactions on online chat rooms. Cryptocurrency investors may choose to hide the profit made from trading by the peer to peer transactions. Some cryptocurrency investors can use sites such as bitcoins mixer, and transaction mixer to hide their bitcoins transactions and wallets.

iii. <u>Wrong transfers are not revertible:</u> Bitcoins wallet is traceable on the blockchain. Some cryptocurrencies have been designed for anonymous transactions and their wallet are not traceable such cryptocurrencies are Monero coins, Dash coins, Verge coins, Z Cash coins, and H Cash coins. Since there are no intermediary financial institutions to transact cryptocurrency if transactions are made with the anonymous coins (Monero, Dash, Verge, Z Cash, and H Cash) and the anonymous coin is mistakenly sent to the wrong wallet it will be difficult to retrieve or revert the coins, this will constitute a loss to a business.

CHAPTER 6

SECURITY IMPLICATIONS

1. Anonymous cryptocurrency coins such as Monero, Dash, etc can be used by criminal-minded individuals to convert illicit funds into cryptocurrency. Illicit fiat money gotten from fraud cripples the economy and businesses are moved secretly through anonymous crypto coins transactions.

2. Some startup agencies or companies have launched their crypto coin during their initial coin offering (ICO) to raise funds for their services, apps, or product but have disappeared after the initial coin offering (ICO) without providing the service they advertised leaving their investors bankrupt and scammed. Typically these offerings involve the opportunity for individual investors to exchange fiat currency such as US dollars or cryptocurrencies (Bitcoin and Ethereum) in return for a digital asset labelled as a coin or token. After the initial coin offering, fraudulent companies disappear and do not list their coin on centralized cryptocurrency exchanges for trading to yield returns on investment.

3. Because Bitcoin is traceable on the blockchain. Some criminal-minded individuals can use sites such as “Bitcoin mixer” to conceal their Bitcoin transaction wallet and identity from accurate monitoring to execute criminal activities such as terrorism financing.

CHAPTER 7

RECOMMENDATIONS

(i) Financial regulatory bodies and security agencies should develop the capacity to monitor and track people who are using cryptocurrency to launder money, scam people, and finance terrorism to foster a peaceful environment for business and economic growth.

(ii) Government should establish a sound fiscal policy position on matters of cryptocurrency trade for the collection of cryptocurrency tax.

(iii) Virtual assets service providers (cryptocurrency exchanges) should be informed to monitor every cryptocurrency transaction and trade to provide identity and details of who sent the crypto coin, the value of the crypto-coin sent, the destination of the crypto coin, and the source of financing for sending the crypto coin, to prevent tax evasion.

(iv) Initial coin offering (ICO) should be registered with the appropriate regulatory agency before commencing sales to the public to checkmate and prevent fraudulent ICOs offered by fraudulent companies.

(v) Lastly, the security agencies should work with certified cryptocurrency forensic investigators to track and trace faces behind cryptocurrency transactions to curb money laundering, terrorism financing and other related crimes which affect the economy.

CHAPTER 8

IMPLEMENTATION STRATEGIES

As earlier stated, security agencies should vigorously act in accordance with the steps aforementioned and in collaboration with policymakers and financial governing bodies relentlessly provide guidance to the government on matters pertaining to fiscal policy formulation for the growth of the economy. Awareness of the new cryptocurrency regulations set up in various countries should be brought to the attention of all cryptocurrency exchange providers and issuers of digital tokens through sensitization programmes.

CHAPTER 9

CONCLUSION

It is clear that cryptocurrency can influence a nation's economy and more people are likely to use cryptocurrency in the nearest future for payment of goods and services worldwide. Cryptocurrency is here to stay, individuals and businesses who are interested in the issuance of cryptocurrency or digital tokens should adhere to the guidelines and rules set up by the regulatory agencies in the country they seek to operate.

ABOUT THE AUTHOR

Ogudo Adaobi Chinenye is a certified and licensed Economics teacher who holds a Bachelor's degree in Education Economics. She has experience in a security organization. Also, she has a background in research Economics. She loves to travel, teach and research.

www.ingramcontent.com/pod-product-compliance
Lightning Source LLC
LaVergne TN
LVHW052115160826
845678LV00015B/3560

* 9 7 9 8 8 4 5 8 5 6 1 1 1 *